hardie grant books
MELBOURNE · LONDON

contents

Basics

Savoury

Sweet

basics

Stovetop popcorn

3 tablespoons vegetable oil
100 g (3½ oz/½ cup) popcorn kernels

Heat the oil in a large heavy-based saucepan over medium–high heat. Add popcorn, and shake to evenly coat the kernels with oil.

Cover the saucepan with a lid and heat for 1–2 minutes, regularly shaking the pan back and forth. After a few minutes, you will hear the popcorn start to pop. Keep shaking the pan until the popping has slowed to once every 2–3 seconds. Remove from the heat, and immediately pour into a large bowl.

Tip: for a delicious buttery flavour, substitute butter for half the oil.

Microwave popcorn

4 tablespoons popcorn kernels
1 teaspoon vegetable oil (optional)

Place the popcorn kernels in a large brown paper bag. Add the oil, if using, and shake the bag to coat the kernels. Fold the top 1 cm (½ in) of the bag over and crease, then repeat two more times. Twist the top corners of the bag to seal.

Microwave the popcorn on high for 2 minutes, listening for the sound of popping kernels. Once the popping has slowed to 2–3 pops a second (this takes roughly 1½ minutes in a 1000-watt microwave), remove the bag from the microwave and immediately pour the popcorn into a large bowl.

savoury

Corn on the cob

100 g (3½ oz) butter, melted
1 x quantity Stovetop popcorn (page 8) or
   2 x quantities Microwave popcorn (page 10)
salt and ground black pepper

Drizzle the butter over the popcorn and
toss to coat. Season with salt and pepper,
and toss again.

Nacho

75 g (2¾ oz) butter
½ teaspoon sweet paprika
½ teaspoon garlic powder
½ teaspoon onion powder
½ teaspoon ground cumin
1 x quantity Stovetop popcorn (page 8) or
   2 x quantities Microwave popcorn (page 10)
salt
50 g (1¾ oz/½ cup) grated parmesan cheese

Melt the butter in a small heavy-based saucepan over medium heat. Remove from the heat and stir in the paprika, garlic powder, onion powder and cumin.

Drizzle the butter mixture over the popcorn, season with salt, and toss to coat. Add the parmesan and toss again.

Greek spiced

1 tablespoon dried dill
1 teaspoon lemon pepper
½ teaspoon onion powder
½ teaspoon dried oregano
1 teaspoon salt
1 x quantity Stovetop popcorn (page 8) or
    2 x quantities Microwave popcorn (page 10)

Combine the dill, lemon pepper,
onion powder, oregano and salt in
a small bowl.

Sprinkle the spice mixture over the
popcorn. Toss to coat.

Pizza-herb

½ teaspoon dried oregano
½ teaspoon dried basil
½ teaspoon garlic powder
½ teaspoon onion powder
¼ teaspoon salt
75 g (2¾ oz) butter
1 teaspoon tomato ketchup
1 x quantity Stovetop popcorn (page 8) or
   2 x quantities Microwave popcorn (page 10)
3 tablespoons finely grated parmesan cheese

Combine the oregano, basil, garlic powder, onion powder and salt in a bowl.

Melt the butter in a small heavy-based saucepan over medium heat. Remove from the heat and stir in the ketchup.

Drizzle the butter mixture over the popcorn and toss to coat. Add the parmesan and herbs and toss again.

Chilli–lime

1 tablespoon palm sugar (jaggery)
2–3 teaspoons chilli flakes
1 tablespoon peanut oil
3 tablespoons lime juice
salt and ground black pepper
1 x quantity Stovetop popcorn (page 8) or
    2 x quantities Microwave popcorn (page 10)

In a small heavy-based saucepan,
combine the palm sugar, chilli flakes, oil,
lime juice, and salt and pepper. Heat over
medium–high heat for about 5 minutes,
stirring occasionally, until the sugar
dissolves and the mixture is well combined.

Drizzle the chilli–lime mixture over the
popcorn. Stir with a wooden spoon to coat.

Lemon

75 g (2¾ oz) butter
juice and finely grated zest of ½ lemon
½ teaspoon chilli powder (optional)
1 x quantity Stovetop popcorn (page 8) or
   2 x quantities Microwave popcorn (page 10)
salt

Melt the butter in a small heavy-based saucepan over medium heat. Remove from the heat and stir in the lemon juice and zest, and chilli powder (if using).

Drizzle the butter mixture over the popcorn, season with salt, and toss to coat.

Salt & vinegar

3 tablespoons vinegar
1 x quantity Stovetop popcorn (page 8) or
   2 x quantities Microwave popcorn (page 10)
salt

Pour the vinegar into a spritzer bottle.

Spritz the popcorn lightly with the vinegar, tossing the popcorn as you go to evenly coat. Season with salt and toss again.

PREMIUM
APPLE CIDER
VINEGAR
Free from artificial colours, flavours and preservatives
750 mL
CONSUMER ADVISORY CENTRE
FREECALL 1800 638 112

Blue cheese

1 x quantity Stovetop popcorn (page 8) or
  2 x quantities Microwave popcorn (page 10)
50 g (1¾ oz) semi-hard blue cheese, frozen
salt and ground black pepper

While the popcorn is still hot, grate the
blue cheese over the top.

Season with salt and pepper, and toss
to coat.

Wasabi

75 g (2¾ oz) butter, melted
3 teaspoons wasabi paste
1 x quantity Stovetop popcorn (page 8) or
   2 x quantities Microwave popcorn (page 10)
salt

Mix the butter with the wasabi in a small
bowl. Stir thoroughly until well combined.

Drizzle the wasabi mixture over the
popcorn. Season with salt and toss
to coat.

Garlic & cayenne pepper

2 garlic cloves, crushed
½ teaspoon cayenne pepper
½ teaspoon salt
75 g (2¾ oz) butter, melted
1 x quantity Stovetop popcorn (page 8) or
    2 x quantities Microwave popcorn (page 10)

Mix the garlic, cayenne pepper, salt and butter together in a small bowl.

Drizzle the butter mixture over the popcorn and toss to coat.

Curry spiced

1 teaspoon curry powder
1 teaspoon turmeric
1 teaspoon salt
2 tablespoons honey
75 g (2¾ oz) butter
1 x quantity Stovetop popcorn (page 8) or
   2 x quantities Microwave popcorn (page 10)

Combine the curry powder, turmeric and salt in a small bowl.

Melt the honey and butter together in a small saucepan over low heat.

Drizzle the honey mixture over the popcorn. Toss to coat. Add the spice mix and toss again.

Parmesan & thyme

75 g (2¾ oz) butter
2 garlic cloves, crushed
2 tablespoons roughly chopped thyme leaves
1 x quantity Stovetop popcorn (page 8) or
    2 x quantities Microwave popcorn (page 10)
50 g (1¾ oz/½ cup) grated parmesan cheese
salt

Melt the butter in a small heavy-based
saucepan over low heat, then add the
garlic and 1 tablespoon of the thyme.
Simmer for 1–2 minutes, until fragrant.

Drizzle the butter mixture over the
popcorn and toss to coat. Add the
parmesan and remaining thyme,
season with salt, and toss again.

Chipotle

3 tablespoons butter
½ teaspoon ground chipotle pepper
¾ teaspoon chilli powder
¾ teaspoon smoked paprika
2 garlic cloves, crushed
1 x quantity Stovetop popcorn (page 8) or
    2 x quantities Microwave popcorn (page 10)
salt

Combine the butter, chipotle, chilli, paprika, and garlic in a small heavy-based saucepan over low heat. Cook for about 5 minutes, stirring regularly.

Drizzle the butter mixture over the popcorn and toss to coat. Season with salt and toss again.

Seaweed

1 sheet nori
¼ teaspoon salt
pinch of chilli flakes (optional)
1 x quantity Stovetop popcorn (page 8) or
    2 x quantities Microwave popcorn (page 10)

Lightly toast the nori by holding over an open flame using a pair of tongs. Toast for about 20 seconds, moving the sheet around so that it toasts evenly.

Break the toasted nori into small pieces, place in a spice grinder or mortar and pestle along with the salt and chilli flakes (if using) then grind to a fine powder.

Sprinkle the nori mixture over the popcorn and toss to coat.

Cajun spiced

1 teaspoon smoked paprika
½ teaspoon onion powder
½ teaspoon garlic powder
¼ teaspoon cayenne pepper
1 teaspoon lemon pepper
½ teaspoon salt
75 g (2¾ oz) butter, melted
1 x quantity Stovetop popcorn (page 8) or
    2 x quantities Microwave popcorn (page 10)

Combine the paprika, onion powder, garlic powder, cayenne pepper, lemon pepper and salt in a small bowl.

Drizzle the butter over the popcorn and toss to coat. Add the spice mix and toss again.

Five-spice

1 x quantity Stovetop popcorn (page 8)
2 tablespoons sugar
1 teaspoon salt
1 teaspoon five-spice powder
1 tablespoon toasted sesame seeds

Cook the popcorn according to the instructions for Stovetop popcorn on page 8, adding the sugar, salt and five-spice powder to the saucepan with the oil.

Sprinkle cooked popcorn with sesame seeds before serving.

Ploughman's

75 g (2¾ oz) butter
½ teaspoon garlic salt
¼ teaspoon onion powder
1 x quantity Stovetop popcorn (page 8) or
   2 x quantities Microwave popcorn (page 10)
3 tablespoons grated parmesan cheese
2 tablespoons fried shallots

Preheat the oven to 160°C (325°F). Line a baking tray with baking paper.

Combine the butter, garlic salt and onion powder in a saucepan over low heat for 5 minutes, stirring regularly.

Drizzle the mixture over the popcorn and toss. Turn the seasoned popcorn onto the baking tray and bake for 7–10 minutes, stirring once. Sprinkle with the parmesan and shallots and toss. Let the popcorn cool, stirring once or twice, before serving.

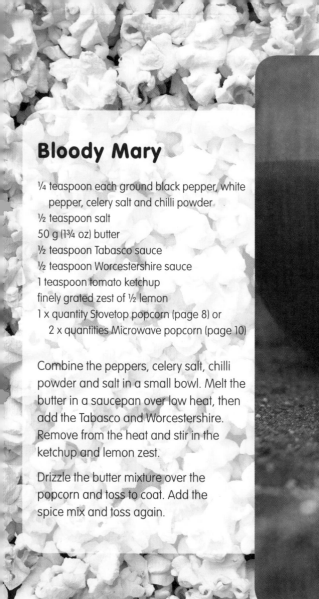

Bloody Mary

¼ teaspoon each ground black pepper, white
   pepper, celery salt and chilli powder
½ teaspoon salt
50 g (1¾ oz) butter
½ teaspoon Tabasco sauce
½ teaspoon Worcestershire sauce
1 teaspoon tomato ketchup
finely grated zest of ½ lemon
1 x quantity Stovetop popcorn (page 8) or
   2 x quantities Microwave popcorn (page 10)

Combine the peppers, celery salt, chilli
powder and salt in a small bowl. Melt the
butter in a saucepan over low heat, then
add the Tabasco and Worcestershire.
Remove from the heat and stir in the
ketchup and lemon zest.

Drizzle the butter mixture over the
popcorn and toss to coat. Add the
spice mix and toss again.

Mexican

75 g (2¾ oz) butter, melted
1 teaspoon smoked paprika
1 teaspoon dried oregano
1 teaspoon ground cumin
½ teaspoon chilli powder
juice and zest from ½ lime
1 x quantity Stovetop popcorn (page 8) or
    2 x quantities Microwave popcorn (page 10)
salt

Melt the butter in a small heavy-based
saucepan over low heat, then add
paprika, oregano, cumin, chilli and lime
zest. Simmer for 1–2 minutes, until
fragrant. Remove from the heat and stir
in the lime juice.

Drizzle the butter mixture over the
popcorn, season with salt, and toss
to coat.

Mustard & cheddar

185 g (6½ oz/1½ cups) finely grated sharp
  cheddar cheese
2 teaspoons poppy seeds
½ teaspoon onion powder
¼ teaspoon mustard powder
75 g (2¾ oz) butter, melted
1 x quantity Stovetop popcorn (page 8) or
  2 x quantities Microwave popcorn (page 10)
salt and ground black pepper

Combine the cheese, poppy seeds,
onion powder and mustard powder
in a small bowl.

Drizzle the melted butter over the
popcorn. Toss to coat. Add the cheese
mix and season with salt and pepper,
and toss again.

Bacon

2 tablespoons oil
2 slices fatty bacon, diced
1 x quantity Stovetop popcorn (page 8)
salt

Heat 1 tablespoon of oil and cook the bacon in a frying pan over medium heat until crisp. Carefully pour the bacon fat into a large heavy-based saucepan and transfer the bacon to paper towel.

Add the remaining oil to the bacon fat and then cook the popcorn in the oil mixture according to the Stovetop popcorn instructions on page 8.

Crumble the crispy bacon pieces over the popcorn, season with salt and toss to coat.

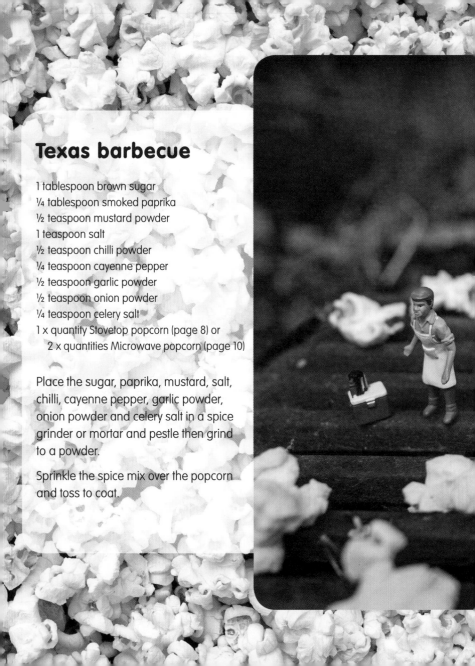

Texas barbecue

1 tablespoon brown sugar
¼ tablespoon smoked paprika
½ teaspoon mustard powder
1 teaspoon salt
½ teaspoon chilli powder
¼ teaspoon cayenne pepper
½ teaspoon garlic powder
½ teaspoon onion powder
¼ teaspoon celery salt
1 x quantity Stovetop popcorn (page 8) or
    2 x quantities Microwave popcorn (page 10)

Place the sugar, paprika, mustard, salt, chilli, cayenne pepper, garlic powder, onion powder and celery salt in a spice grinder or mortar and pestle then grind to a powder.

Sprinkle the spice mix over the popcorn and toss to coat.

Moroccan spiced

½ teaspoon ground ginger
½ teaspoon ground cardamom
½ teaspoon ground cumin
¼ teaspoon cinnamon
¼ teaspoon ground allspice
¼ teaspoon ground coriander
¼ teaspoon nutmeg
¼ teaspoon turmeric
pinch of ground black pepper
75 g (2¾ oz) butter, melted
1 x quantity Stovetop popcorn (page 8) or
    2 x quantities Microwave popcorn (page 10)

Combine all of the spices in a bowl.

Drizzle the butter over the popcorn and
toss to coat. Sprinkle with the spice mix
and toss again.

Burnt butter & sage

75 g (2¾ oz) butter
small handful sage leaves
salt and ground black pepper
1 x quantity Stovetop popcorn (page 8) or
    2 x quantities Microwave popcorn (page 10)

Melt the butter in a small heavy-based saucepan over medium heat, then add the sage leaves. Cook for 4–5 minutes, swirling the pan often, until sage leaves are crisp and the butter has turned a deep nut-brown colour. Season with salt and pepper.

Drizzle the butter mixture over the popcorn and toss to coat.

Vanilla

1 x quantity Stovetop popcorn (page 8)
1 vanilla bean, split lengthwise
30 g (1 oz) unsalted butter
1 tablespoon caster (superfine) sugar
salt to taste

Cook the popcorn according to the
Stovetop popcorn instructions on page 8,
adding the vanilla bean to the saucepan
with the popcorn kernels.

Remove the vanilla bean from the popped
popcorn and scrape the seeds into a
small heavy-based saucepan. Add the
butter, sugar and salt and cook for about
5 minutes, stirring regularly.

Drizzle the butter mixture over the
popcorn and toss to coat.

Choc peanut butter

170 g (6 oz) dark (semisweet) chocolate,
  chopped
3 tablespoons unsalted butter
125 g (4 oz/½ cup) peanut butter
1 teaspoon natural vanilla extract
1 x quantity Stovetop popcorn (page 8) or
    2 x quantities Microwave popcorn (page 10)
185 g (6½ oz/1½ cups) icing (confectioners')
  sugar

Grease and line a baking tray with baking
paper. Place the chocolate, butter and
peanut butter in a double boiler and stir
gently until melted and smooth. Remove
from the heat and stir in the vanilla.

Pour the chocolate mixture over the
popcorn and stir to coat. Sift the icing
sugar over the top and stir again. Spread
onto the prepared baking tray and
refrigerate for about 30 minutes until set,
before breaking into pieces.

Maple bacon

2 slices bacon
1 x quantity Stovetop popcorn (page 8)
60 g (2 oz) butter
115 g (4 oz/½ cup) brown sugar
3 tablespoons maple syrup
2 tablespoons bourbon
1 teaspoon natural vanilla extract
⅛ teaspoon bicarb soda (baking soda)
salt

Preheat oven to 120°C. Grease and line a
baking tray with baking paper. In a frying
pan, fry the bacon until crisp. Drain on
kitchen paper, then crumble over the
popcorn. Set aside. Combine the butter,
sugar and maple syrup in a saucepan over
medium heat. Cook, stirring constantly, until
the sugar dissolves. Bring to the boil, then
reduce the heat and simmer without stirring
for about 5 minutes, until golden. Remove
from the heat and mix in the bourbon,
vanilla, bicarb soda and salt. Pour the
caramel over the popcorn and stir to coat.
Spread onto the tray and sprinkle with salt
then bake, stirring every 15 minutes, for
1 hour. Allow to cool completely.

KEEJ

Maple Farm

100% Pure

Maple Syr

CANADA No

Medium

PAREVE
MK
511

189 ml (250 g)

Rocky road

100 g (3½ oz) milk chocolate
2 tablespoons unsalted butter
50 g (1¾ oz) roasted peanuts, chopped
2 tablespoons chopped glacé cherries
50 g (1¾ oz/1 cup) mini marshmallows
1 x quantity Stovetop popcorn (page 8) or
   2 x quantities Microwave popcorn (page 10)

Grease and line a baking tray with baking paper.

Place the chocolate and butter in a double boiler and stir gently until melted and smooth. Remove from the heat and stir in the peanuts and glacé cherries.

Combine the popcorn and marshmallows. Pour the chocolate mixture over the popcorn and stir to coat. Spread onto the prepared baking tray and refrigerate for about 30 minutes until the chocolate has set, before breaking into pieces.

Cinnamon

75 g (2½ oz) unsalted butter
110 g (4 oz/½ cup) sugar
3 teaspoons cinnamon
½ teaspoon salt
1 x quantity Stovetop popcorn (page 8) or
    2 x quantities Microwave popcorn (page 10)

Combine the butter, sugar, cinnamon and salt in a small heavy-based saucepan over low heat. Cook for about 5 minutes, stirring regularly.

Drizzle the butter mixture over the popcorn and toss to coat.

Sugar & spice

3 tablespoons caster (superfine) sugar
½–1 teaspoon chilli powder
1 x quantity Stovetop popcorn (page 8) or
    2 x quantities Microwave popcorn (page 10)

Place the sugar and chilli powder in a
spice grinder or mortar and pestle then
grind to a powder.

Sprinkle the sugar mix over the popcorn
and toss to coat.

Mojito

3 tablespoons sugar
½ teaspoon salt
zest of 1 lime, grated
4 mint leaves
30 g (1 oz) butter, melted
1 x quantity Stovetop popcorn (page 8) or
    2 x quantities Microwave popcorn (page 10)

Place the sugar, salt, lime zest and mint
leaves in a food processor and process to
a fine powder.

Drizzle the butter over the popcorn and
toss to coat. Sprinkle with the mojito sugar
and toss again.

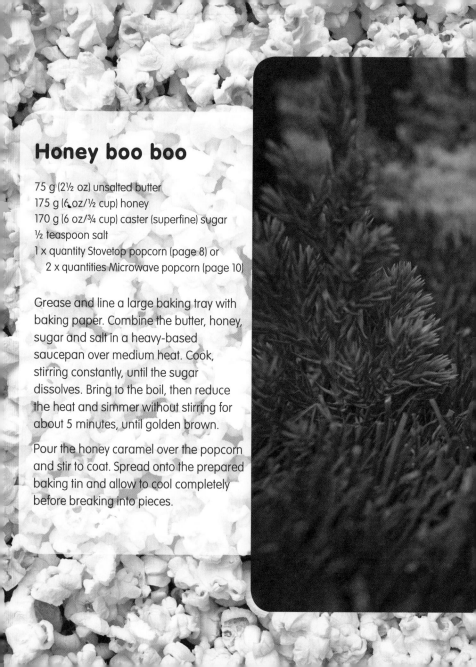

Honey boo boo

75 g (2½ oz) unsalted butter
175 g (6 oz/½ cup) honey
170 g (6 oz/¾ cup) caster (superfine) sugar
½ teaspoon salt
1 x quantity Stovetop popcorn (page 8) or
   2 x quantities Microwave popcorn (page 10)

Grease and line a large baking tray with baking paper. Combine the butter, honey, sugar and salt in a heavy-based saucepan over medium heat. Cook, stirring constantly, until the sugar dissolves. Bring to the boil, then reduce the heat and simmer without stirring for about 5 minutes, until golden brown.

Pour the honey caramel over the popcorn and stir to coat. Spread onto the prepared baking tin and allow to cool completely before breaking into pieces.

Pistachio praline

770 g (1 lb 11 oz/3½ cups) sugar
140 g (5 oz) unsalted butter, cubed
150 g (5½ oz/1 cup) shelled, dry-roasted
   pistachios, roughly chopped
1 teaspoon cider vinegar
1 teaspoon salt
1 x quantity Stovetop popcorn (page 8) or
   2 x quantities Microwave popcorn (page 10)

Grease and line a baking tray with baking paper. Heat the sugar in a dry, large heavy-based saucepan over medium heat, stirring constantly with a fork. Once the sugar starts to melt, stop stirring and leave it to cook, swirling the pan occasionally, until the caramel is a deep golden brown.

Reduce the heat to low and stir in the butter, pistachios, vinegar and salt. When the butter has melted, add the popcorn and stir to coat. Spread onto the prepared baking tray and press down with a spatula. Allow to cool completely before cutting or breaking into pieces.

Candy

110 g (4 oz) boiled sweets (rock candy)
300 g (10½ oz) milk chocolate, chopped
1 x quantity Stovetop popcorn (page 8) or
    2 x quantities Microwave popcorn (page 10)

Line a large baking tray with baking paper. Seal the sweets in a zip-lock bag and crush with a rolling pin. Set aside.

Place the chocolate in a double boiler and stir gently until melted and smooth.

In a large bowl, combine the crushed sweets and popcorn. Pour the melted chocolate over the top and stir to coat. Spread onto the prepared baking tray and refrigerate for about 30 minutes until the chocolate has set, before breaking into pieces.

Caramel

115 g (4 oz) unsalted butter
115 g (4 oz/½ cup) caster (superfine) sugar
3 tablespoons brown sugar
1 teaspoon salt
½ teaspoon bicarb soda (baking soda)
½ teaspoon vanilla essence
1 x quantity Stovetop popcorn (page 8) or
   2 x quantities Microwave popcorn (page 10)

Preheat oven to 140°C. Grease and line a baking tray with baking paper. Combine the butter, sugars and salt in a saucepan over medium heat. Cook, stirring constantly, until the sugar dissolves. Bring to the boil, then reduce the heat and simmer without stirring for about 5 minutes, until golden brown. Remove from the heat and mix in the bicarb soda and vanilla.

Pour the caramel over the popcorn and stir to coat. Spread onto the prepared baking tray and bake, stirring every 15 minutes, for 45 minutes. Allow to cool completely before breaking into pieces.

Rainbow

1 x quantity Stovetop popcorn (page 8) or
    2 x quantities Microwave popcorn (page 10)
165 g (5½ oz/¾ cup) sugar
food colouring in 3 different colours

Divide the popcorn between three large
bowls. Grease and line three baking trays
with baking paper.

Combine the sugar with 3 tablespoons
water in a medium heavy-based
saucepan over medium heat. Cook,
stirring constantly, until the sugar
dissolves. Bring to the boil, then reduce
the heat and simmer without stirring for
about 2 minutes, or until the syrup has
thickened.

Divide the syrup between three bowls and
stir in a few drops of food colouring.

Pour each coloured syrup over a bowl of
popcorn and stir to coat. Spread onto the
prepared baking trays and leave to
harden before combining.

Coconut rough

170 g (6 oz) dark (semisweet) chocolate, chopped
3 tablespoons butter
1 tablespoon milk
1 x quantity Stovetop popcorn (page 8) or
  2 x quantities Microwave popcorn (page 10)
½ cup shredded coconut, toasted

Grease and line a baking tray with baking paper. Make a double boiler by setting a heatproof bowl over a saucepan of hot water over low–medium heat. The bowl should fit snugly and not touch the water. Place the chocolate, butter and milk in the bowl and stir gently until melted and smooth.

Combine the popcorn and coconut. Pour the chocolate mixture over the popcorn and stir to coat. Spread onto the prepared baking tray and refrigerate for about 30 minutes until the chocolate has set, before breaking into pieces.

Marshmallow

100 g (3½ oz) butter
115 g (4 oz/½ cup) brown sugar
250 g (9 oz) marshmallows
1 x quantity Stovetop popcorn (page 8) or
   2 x quantities Microwave popcorn (page 10)

Grease and line a baking tray with baking paper. Combine the butter and sugar in a large saucepan over low heat. Stir until the butter has melted and the sugar has dissolved. Add the marshmallows and cook, stirring often, for 5–7 minutes until the marshmallows have melted and the mixture is thin enough to pour.

Pour the marshmallow mixture over the popcorn and stir to coat. Spread out onto the prepared baking tray and allow to cool for 10 minutes before eating.

Choc cherry

4 tablespoons kirsch or other cherry liqueur
220 g (8 oz) dark chocolate, chopped
3 tablespoons chopped glacé (candied) cherries
90 g (3 oz/1 cup) shredded coconut, toasted
½ teaspoon salt
1 x quantity Stovetop popcorn (page 8) or
    2 x quantities Microwave popcorn (page 10)

Line a large baking tray with baking
paper. Heat the kirsch in a small
saucepan over low heat until it reaches
simmering point.

Place the chocolate and kirsch in a double
boiler and stir gently until melted and
smooth. Remove from the heat and mix
in the glacé cherries.

In a large bowl, combine the coconut, salt
and popcorn. Pour the chocolate mixture
over the popcorn and stir to coat. Spread
onto the prepared baking tray and
refrigerate for about 30 minutes until set,
before breaking into pieces.

Mocha

330 g (11½ oz/1½ cups) sugar
2 tablespoons unsweetened cocoa powder,
   sifted
2 teaspoons instant coffee granules
125 ml (4 fl oz/½ cup) milk
1 x quantity Stovetop popcorn (page 8) or
   2 x quantities Microwave popcorn (page 10)

Grease and line 3 baking trays with
baking paper. Combine the sugar, cocoa,
coffee and milk in a medium heavy-
based saucepan over medium heat.
Cook, stirring constantly, until the sugar
dissolves. Bring to the boil, then reduce
the heat and simmer without stirring for
about 2 minutes, or until the syrup has
thickened.

Pour the mixture over the popcorn and stir
to coat. Spread onto the prepared baking
tray and allow to cool before breaking
into pieces.

Published in 2013 by Hardie Grant Books

Hardie Grant Books (Australia)
Ground Floor, Building 1
658 Church Street
Richmond, Victoria 3121
www.hardiegrant.com.au

Hardie Grant Books (UK)
Dudley House, North Suite
34–35 Southampton Street
London WC2E 7HF
www.hardiegrant.co.uk

POP!
ISBN 9781742706115

Publishing Director: Paul McNally
Project Editor: Hannah Koelmeyer
Design Manager: Heather Menzies
Photographer: Hannah Koelmeyer
Production Manager: Todd Rechner

Colour reproduction by Splitting Image Colour Studio
Printed and bound in China by 1010 Printing International Limited

Please note: 1 tablespoon is equivalent to 4 teaspoons.